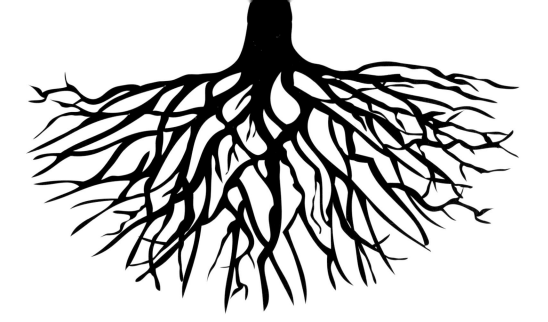

BRANCHING OUT

HOW TREES *are* *part of* OUR WORLD

by JOAN MARIE GALAT

Owl kids

For Amy, who walked beneath a black bear in a tree.

Text © 2014 Joan Marie Galat

Owlkids Books acknowledges the financial support of the Canada Council for the Arts, the Ontario Arts Council, the Government of Canada through the Canada Book Fund (CBF) and the Government of Ontario through the Ontario Media Development Corporation's Book Initiative for our publishing activities.

Published in Canada by
Owlkids Books Inc.
10 Lower Spadina Avenue
Toronto, ON M5V 2Z2

Published in the United States by
Owlkids Books Inc.
1700 Fourth Street
Berkeley, CA 94710

Library and Archives Canada Cataloguing in Publication

Galat, Joan Marie, 1963-, author
    Branching out : how trees are part of our world / by Joan Marie Galat.

Includes index.
ISBN 978-1-77147-049-0 (bound).--ISBN 978-1-77147-082-7 (pbk.)

    1. Trees--Juvenile literature. I. Title.

QK475.8.G34 2014   j582.16   C2014-900388-9

Library of Congress Control Number: 2014932714

Edited by: Jennifer Stokes and Jessica Burgess
Illustrations by: Wendy Ding

Manufactured in Shen Zhen, Guang Dong, in May 2014, by Printplus Limited
Job #7273

A   B   C   D   E   F

MIX
Paper from
responsible sources
FSC® C018479

 Publisher of Chirp, chickaDEE and OWL
www.owlkidsbooks.com

Contents

Why you need trees

Trees have been around for nearly 400 million years, and today from 25,000 to 100,000 species are believed to exist, with new species often being discovered. You couldn't claim to have seen every kind of tree. But you could claim with certainty that trees touch your daily life either through the products they provide, the habitats they create, the animals they support, or the feelings they inspire.

Even though you live in an ecosystem sustained by trees, their impact on daily life is not always obvious. Imagine for a moment what life would be like if you took away all the trees. You wouldn't have a stick inside your Popsicle, a book, or a house. You would not play with cards, wrap presents in paper, or ride a skateboard. You would never pour maple syrup on waffles, bite into apples, drink lemonade, or crack walnuts. You would not have bulletin boards, cellophane, egg cartons, life jackets, natural rubber erasers, sandpaper, or twine. There would be no leafy shade, no campfires, no hockey sticks.

Your environment is more stable and safe thanks to forests, which help prevent flooding by soaking up extra water after it rains. Leafy trees and fallen leaves slow the force of rain and the speed at which rain enters the soil. This helps rainwater drip into the ground, instead of washing across the surface and carrying soil away. Rows of trees make windbreaks that help keep soil

The world's oldest tree is a bristlecone pine growing in California's Ancient Bristlecone Pine Forest. Named Methuselah, the more than 4,700-year-old tree is still growing. But no sign identifies the tree, in order to protect it from vandalism and souvenir seekers.

in place, slow cold winds, and stop other plants from becoming too dry. Tree roots clean soil by filtering ground and surface water pollution caused by fertilizers and pesticides.

Without trees, every animal species that depends on a tree habitat to survive could become extinct. With fewer carnivorous birds, farmland pests like mice and certain insects would thrive. You would lose clean air, and the world would be a noisier place, for leaves filter air and trees muffle sound.

Fortunately, trees do exist. They are the giants of the plant world, and some species live for thousands of years. Ancient trees that still survive may have sheltered indigenous tribes, early explorers, and ancient armies. Both heroes and villains of history have used trees for fuel, food, medicines, and building materials. Trees have provided timber for castles and gallows, drumsticks and drums, and planks to build the railway that opened up North America. A renewable resource, trees continue to provide materials people depend on, as well as something more difficult to measure—human joy. Trees inspire a sense of peace and belonging with the natural world. That's a fancy way of saying that trees make you feel good!

Trees belong to communities in nature called ecosystems—places where plants and animals interact with each other to live and grow. Tree habitats provide animals with food, shelter, and nesting materials.

TREE FACT

Even a dead tree is a valuable part of the ecosystem. Fallen branches, logs, and snags—standing dead trees—provide mammals with shelter and birds with places to nest and perch. Sometimes trees grow out of a nurse log—a fallen tree that provides the nutrition and moisture a tree seedling needs to take root.

Global warming

If you've ever stepped into a garden greenhouse or a car that's been sitting in the sunlight with the windows up, you know how unpleasant too much hot air can feel. Parking a car under a shady tree makes the temperature much more bearable!

In the same way that car windows and greenhouse walls hold heat, the Earth's atmosphere traps warm air around our planet. Carbon dioxide and other heat-trapping gases—called greenhouse gases—collect in the atmosphere. When more of these gases build up, less heat can radiate into space and the Earth grows warmer and warmer. This phenomenon, called global warming, causes temperatures to rise, and snow, sea ice, and glaciers to melt.

Excess greenhouse gases are generated by human activity like burning fossil fuels—coal, oil, and natural gas. When people plant trees, global warming is reduced because trees remove carbon dioxide from the air. They store the carbon dioxide and use it to grow roots, leaves, flowers, bark, and wood. Trees also help lower air temperatures through the transpiration process—when the water drawn up through a tree's roots evaporates through its leaves. But when people cut down trees or burn deadfall, more carbon dioxide stays in the Earth's atmosphere.

Global warming is a problem that affects all

Keeping our forests healthy and full is one of the most important ways we can reduce the buildup of CO_2 in the atmosphere.

Photosynthesis
Trees need carbon dioxide to live, just as we need oxygen to live. Through photosynthesis—the process of converting light energy into chemical energy—trees remove carbon dioxide from the air and release oxygen back into it. In photosynthesis, a tree's leaves combine light, water, and carbon dioxide to make the food trees need to live.

ecosystems. Warmer temperatures increase smog and trigger severe weather like heat waves, wildfires, tornadoes, hurricanes, floods, and heavy rainfall. Higher temperatures can make habitats become unsuitable for agriculture. Global warming also causes sea levels to rise. As shorelines become affected by thermal expansion—warm water taking up more space than cold water—the increase can mean that expensive bridges, roads, reservoirs, dams, and ports have to be altered or replaced.

Since the early 1990s, sea levels have risen 0.14 inches (3.5 millimeters) every year. That doesn't sound like much, but it's enough to impact coastal habitats through flooding, freshwater contamination, and loss of wildlife habitat and farmland. If sea levels rise 3 feet (1 meter), nearly 56 million people will need to move to higher ground. Since trees absorb water, planting them in floodplains—low areas where floods are likely to occur—helps lower the impact of too much water collecting in one place.

Coniferous Tree

Deciduous Tree

Have you seen my leaves?

Trees are sorted into groups according to how they reproduce, the types of leaves they grow, and when they lose their leaves. Coniferous trees grow cones, and most produce leaves that are needles. Deciduous trees, like the red maple, grow broad leaves each spring and drop their leaves in the autumn. Some trees, like the coniferous Scotch pine, are also called evergreens because they lose and replace their needles gradually instead of all at once.

Every part of a tree has a purpose

Each tree species has a particular leaf shape, flower type, bark thickness, root system, and other characteristics that enable it to survive in a particular environment.

1 CROWN: The crown includes all of the tree's twigs, branches, and leaves. The crown's shape, which may be rounded, conical, spreading, or another form, changes as the tree grows.

2 LEAVES: Leaves make all the food plants need to live. They produce food through photosynthesis. Just like us, plants eat, drink, and breathe. But, unlike us, they have to meet their needs without moving from place to place. Plants make the sugar they need for food by using three things they can get from one spot—light, water, and carbon dioxide.

3 FLOWERS/FRUIT/SEEDS: Trees reproduce by growing flowers or cones that produce many different types of fruits and seeds. You may see nuts or winged seeds on some trees, but others might generate their seeds inside fruits, cones, pods, or capsules.

4 BRANCHES: Branches support twigs, leaves, and flowers, in addition to providing habitats for lichens and other plants.

5 SAP: This watery solution of dissolved sugar, salt, and minerals moves through a tree's tissues to bring nourishment to the roots, trunk, branches, and leaves.

6 TRUNK: Also called a bole, the trunk forms the main stem of the tree from the ground to the branches. The trunk supports the tree's weight.

7 BARK: A tree's outer bark helps protect it from extreme temperatures, varying weather conditions, and injury from insects.

8 ROOTS: Roots anchor trees into the ground, as well as absorb moisture and nutrients.

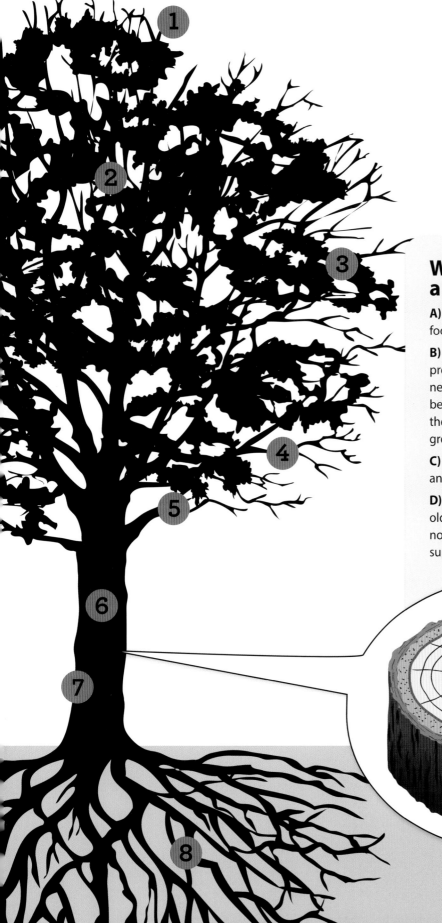

What's underneath a tree's bark?

A) Phloem: The inner bark that transports food from the leaves to the rest of the tree.

B) Cambium: Where cells grow outward to produce new phloem and inward to produce new wood. The ages of some tree species can be determined by counting growth rings—the layer of wood formed during one growing season.

C) Sapwood: Living wood that stores food and transports sap upward from the roots.

D) Heartwood: Sapwood that has become old, hard, and resistant to decay. Although no longer living, it is very strong and helps support the tree's weight.

How to use this book

LEAF SILHOUETTE
The shapes of leaves across species are extremely diverse.

Common Name

Each tree is most often known by a common name, not its scientific name. People living in different regions may use different common names for the same tree species.

(Latin name)

The scientific, or Latin, name is the formal, technical name for each tree. It's composed by listing a Latin form of the tree's genus followed by its species. The genus is a more broad classification, referring to a group of related species that share common characteristics, while the species is more particular. (The same naming system is used for animals too—people belong to the genus *Homo* and the species *sapiens*.)

Pau Brasil
(Caesalpinia echinata)

Brazil is the only country named after a tree. The word "pau" means wood and "brasil" means ember.

20

MAP
The native countries of each tree are highlighted in orange. Some trees now grow outside these countries, but to understand how each tree came to be a vital part of human and animal lives, it's best to start with its native range.

Color helps you tell the difference between sport teams, distinguish between product brands, and show patriotism on a country's flag. Throughout history, color has been used to indicate prestige and wealth: before ~es became commonplace, only the rich could afford the luxury dyed fabrics, and commoners were stuck with drab colors like ~ay and brown. Color is one of the reasons the pau brasil tree in ~azil is now a threatened species.

Exploitation of the pau brasil began in 1501 after Portuguese ~plorers first set foot on the landmass now known as Brazil. ~eking natural resources for their king, explorers met ~asileiros—indigenous people who collected pau brasil wood ~ make a red dye. The dye—a shade like the red of glowing ~nbers—was ideal for coloring textiles. The explorers sent log ~mples home and commercial harvest began, the trees so ~luable they had to be defended against sea pirates. The newly ~scovered land was plundered for this valuable tree, and by the ~ghteenth century tree populations were already falling.

A rare, slow-growing species, pau brasil trees are only native ~ Brazil's threatened Atlantic Coastal Forest—an isolated tropical ~ainforest, originally about twice the size of Texas. Today only ~out 15 percent of the original forest remains. The pau brasil, ~so called pernambuco, prefers low-lying coastal areas with ~ell-drained soils and open forest—woods where trees are not ~owded too close together. Typically a medium-sized tree, pau ~rasil may grow 50 to 60 feet (15 to 18 meters) high and achieve ~trunk 3 feet (1 meter) in diameter. Although a protected ~ecies, the pau brasil is still being harvested illegally.

The pau brasil grows stalks of deep yellow flowers, with ~ne splash of red. They open at dawn and bloom for one day. ~ees, attracted to the sweet-smelling blossoms, pollinate the ~owers, which evolve into oval-shaped seedpods. The woody ~eedpods hang empty upon the tree after twisting open to ~elease their seeds.

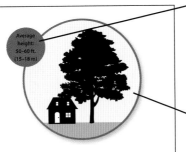

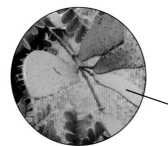

A member of the pea family, the pau brasil grows flat seedpods, about the size of an adult's ear. Small thorns cover the leaves, as well as the seedpods, which contain 2–3 brownish seeds.

Spines on the trunk make this tree hard to climb.

Average height: 50–60 ft. (15–18 m)

AVERAGE HEIGHT
The ranges of tree heights are quite broad, as so many environmental and social factors affect their ages.

SCALE
Each tree is shown to scale at its average height next to an average two-storey house—just under 23 feet (7 meters).

A CLOSER LOOK
These spots outline distinguishing features of each tree.

TREE FACT
Trees create places that allow different types of vegetation to grow. The pau brasil provides important ~abitats for orchids, as well as epiphytes—moss, lichens, and ~ther species that grow on plants.

TREE FACT
Each of these boxes explores an amazing aspect of the specific tree in the chapter or of trees in general.

WHEN YOU PLANT A TREE
These boxes highlight the benefits of planting trees.

Red Maple
(*Acer rubrum*)

The red maple grows in eastern Canada and the Maritimes, and south to eastern Florida and Texas.

The red maple is like a fortune-teller. Its showy red flowers bloom before any leaves appear, a sure sign that spring is on its way. After summer's end, red maples stand out once more as their green leaves turn yellow, orange, or scarlet. Red maple landscapes are so beautiful that people will travel long distances to enjoy their brilliant colors. Luckily, the show lasts for several weeks, only ending when the brightly colored leaves of this deciduous species fall to the ground.

Although considered medium-sized trees, red maples are one of the largest spring-flowering species. They can grow 2 to 5 feet (0.5 to 1.5 meters) per year, reach heights of around 90 feet (27 meters) and diameters of around 24 inches (60 centimeters), and live 80 to 100 years. The roots of the red maple can form a network so dense that other plants are unable to grow near their trunks. One of the most plentiful eastern North American trees, red maples grow in most types of soil and even thrive in wetlands, sometimes forming maple swamps.

Maple blossoms turn into red, pink, or yellow single-seeded fruits called samaras, also known as maple keys. A dry seed forms on one end of the samara, and a papery wing on the other. When wind catches their boomerang-shaped wings, samaras blow to new ground and may sprout immediately or the following spring. Once a red maple's trunk reaches a diameter of 12 inches (30 centimeters), the tree can grow nearly a million seeds a year.

North America is home to thirteen of the approximately one hundred and fifty known species of maple. Ten species grow in Canada, and native maples can be found in every province. A maple leaf was added to the Canadian flag in 1965; however, it may have been used as a Canadian symbol as early as 1700. The red maple is also called Carolina red maple, Drummond red maple, scarlet maple, shoe-pet maple, soft maple, swamp maple, and water maple.

TREE FACT As autumn nights get longer, deciduous leaves begin to die, and sap is no longer transported to leaves. The leaves eventually fall and the tree enters a dormant stage, allowing it to survive the harsher conditions of winter.

Average height: 90 ft. (27 m)

After about four years, young red maples start producing fruits. Maple samaras are sometimes called helicopters or whirlybirds because of the way they spin through the air.

With age, the smooth silver-gray bark of young trees forms dark furrowed ridges.

Before being tapped, trees should be 10–12 inches (25–30 centimeters) in diameter, when measured 4.5 feet (1.4 meters) above the ground.

It takes 43 US gallons (163 liters) of sap to make 1 US gallon (3.8 liters) of syrup, which can be further processed to make maple sugar, fudge, nougat, cream, or candy.

People need red maple trees

Suppose you wanted to celebrate Arbor Day by honoring the red maple. You might sit under its shady branches, at a table made of maple wood, while eating waffles dripping with maple syrup!

The fine-grained wood of the red maple is used in building products and household items, as well as for fuel, sawtimber, and pulp. Pioneers used its wood to build furniture and its bark to make dyes and ink. Indigenous North Americans used maple wood to make carvings, bowls, and spoons, and steeped its bark to make a medicine to treat sore eyes. Today, red maples are often planted as ornamental trees because they are easy to grow, provide shade, and look majestic.

In late winter and early spring, before any buds emerge, sap can be collected to make maple syrup. The sap must be harvested when daytime temperatures are above freezing, but nighttime temperatures go below freezing. A small hole, no more than 3 inches (7.5 centimeters) deep, is drilled into the trunk. The sap drips into a bucket, which hangs from a spout inserted into the hole. One tap might collect 6 to 10 US gallons (23 to 38 liters) of sap, which is then boiled down to make syrup. Red maple is one of many maple species that can be tapped for its sap.

Red maple trees provide shelter for animals like this big brown bat.

Leaves attract katydids looking for places to lay eggs.

Animals need red maple trees

Hands cling to bark as you heave your body up into the limbs of a glorious red maple. A springtime climb might have you dodging honeybees, bumblebees, and other insects visiting pollen-rich flowers. Fluttering mourning cloaks sip nectar, while other butterflies and moths wait for leaves to erupt before coming for a nibble.

Nesting season will bring the *rat-a-tat-tat* of pileated woodpeckers, common flickers, and yellow-bellied sapsuckers. Wood ducks, screech owls, and eastern bluebirds might use these cavities to raise their young, while grosbeaks and other birds come to eat the red maple's plentiful seeds, find shelter, or build a nest.

Hear that rustling below the tree? Perhaps a spotted salamander is hiding in the leaf litter, or an eastern chipmunk is lining its burrow with leaves. Animals like gray squirrels are easier to spot, as they chatter and dash about to gather and store red maple seeds.

You can see where whitetail deer, moose, and elk have browsed by looking for broken tips on tree branches. Check even lower to see where snowshoe hare feed on the sprouts erupting from the trunk.

Better climb down that tree now. A black rat snake is about to slither up to find rodents for its supper!

When you plant a red maple, you plant a tree that is deciduous and therefore particularly good at removing carbon from the atmosphere when it's young.

Banyan
(Ficus benghalensis)

The banyan tree is found in Bangladesh, India, Pakistan, and Sri Lanka monsoon and rainforests.

Average height: 100 ft. (30 m)

Almost every banyan begins with a hungry bird, bat, or monkey that eats a fig and releases a seed-filled dropping onto an upper branch of a tree. Banyans begin life as epiphytes (EP-ih-fites)—plants that sprout on host trees, taking moisture and nutrition from air and rain. The sapling sends roots winding around the trunk and to the ground, where it anchors into the soil. These roots become sturdy trunks that grow limbs. New branches send down additional roots, creating more and more tree trunks.

Over a period of time, sometimes several decades, a banyan tree kills its host tree. Its network of roots gradually strangles the host tree, which can no longer draw nutrients from the ground. Also, the new tree's thick, waxy leaves form an umbrella that blocks sunlight from the host. Sometimes a hollow trunk is all that remains.

Banyan tree flowers grow inside cherry-sized figs. Not true fruit, the figs are really capsules that enclose collections of hundreds of miniature flowers. Only one species of insect can pollinate the flowers—agaonid wasps, also called fig wasps. Smaller than a grain of rice, they are just the right size to enter the tiny opening on one end of a fig. While laying eggs inside the fig, female wasps spread pollen and fertilize the flowers. After the young wasps hatch and exit, a protein-digesting enzyme in the capsule gets rid of any dead wasps or remaining eggs. The pollinated flowers become seeds, and the hard, green figs ripen to a bright red.

Banyan seeds have a greater chance of sprouting after passing through the digestive system of a bird, like this Indian myna.

Evergreen, fast growing, and resistant to drought, banyan trees have the ability to store extra water in their trunks. These long-living trees can reach heights of 100 feet (30 meters) and diameters of nearly 700 feet (213 meters). The Great Banyan at the Indian Botanic Garden in Howrah is one of the largest trees in the world. It has more than 2,800 prop roots over a 3.5-acre (1.5-hectare) area.

The national tree of India and a sacred tree in India and Pakistan, the banyan tree is said to represent eternal life. In some places, people will not cut down a banyan tree or plant crops close to where it grows. The banyan tree is known as the wish-fulfilling tree, the tree of knowledge, and the strangler fig.

The banyan's roots strangle the host tree.

TREE FACT
Starting their lives high above the ground as epiphytes allows banyan saplings to enjoy a well-lit habitat, protected from floods and ground fire. They also escape herbivores, like elephants, who like to feed on their leaves and stems.

Banyan trees serve as a place to stay cool while hanging out.

People need banyan trees

In India, if you plan to meet your friends "under the banyan tree," you might find yourself sharing the space. Banyan trees are such a central point in rural Indian communities that even village council meetings may be held there. As well as providing much-needed shade, banyan leaves are sometimes harvested for animal fodder. The leaves also help reduce noise and air pollution.

Banyans have hard wood that can be made into furniture. The strong aerial roots are used to make rope, tent poles, and cart yokes, while the bark is used to make rope and paper. Banyan wood is also made into pulp and paper, and its milky sap collected to make rubber. The sap is handy as a polish for copper, brass, and bronze objects, too.

One type of bug that lives on banyan trees is called a lac insect. It secretes a substance (lac) that can be collected to make dye and shellac. Lac-encrusted twigs are cut from the tree, then lac is scraped off the branches. As well as being an ingredient in crayons, lipstick, and hair spray, shellac is used as an adhesive, primer, and sealer. You may have eaten products covered with the shellac of lac insects. It is often used to coat candy, and shellac-coated pills are much easier to swallow.

What starts as one banyan tree can grow and spread across large areas of land.

Tiny agaonid wasps carefully make their way into a fig.

The short-nosed fruit bat uses its sense of smell to find figs.

Animals need banyan trees

People are not the only creatures taking advantage of banyan trees. In addition to the tiny agaonid wasps, birds and bats also wing their way to this tree, while spotted deer, nilgai, small Indian civets, and even wild boars browse below.

It's a good thing banyan figs grow year round. The rhesus monkey, Hanuman langur, and hoolock gibbon are three primates that climb the banyan for figs. Bonnet macaques, monkeys that look like they're wearing hats, come to eat as well as to sleep.

Birds abound. You might glimpse yellow-footed green pigeons, long-tailed parakeets, and jungle babblers. If you hear a bird mimicking you, look for a myna bird. The one with a yellow beak and eye patch is a jungle myna. If you see a bird with an ivory-colored casque—a horny helmet-like growth on its bill—it's the Oriental pied hornbill. And if you spot a Malabar pied hornbill, with its mostly black casque, you're lucky. This species is close to being classified as threatened because of habitat loss.

Visit a banyan at night to try to see another species struggling with habitat loss—the sloth bear. Listen for its grunt and snort as it feeds on figs. You might also hear the *whooaa* of a mottled wood owl perched on a branch, or the squabble of a flying fox—a giant fruit bat with a six-foot (2-meter) wing span. Now cover your head—you don't want a fig-eating animal to plant a banyan seed on you!

When you plant a banyan tree, you make a place where people may one day meet up, watch wildlife, and enjoy shade. Historically, the British named these banyan trees for the Hindu merchants called "banians," who peddled their goods under the shade of these giant trees.

Pau Brasil
(*Caesalpinia echinata*)

Brazil is the only country named after a tree. The word "pau" means wood and "brasil" means ember.

Average height: 50–60 ft. (15–18 m)

Color helps you tell the difference between sport teams, distinguish between product brands, and show patriotism on a country's flag. Throughout history, color has been used to indicate prestige and wealth: before dyes became commonplace, only the rich could afford the luxury of dyed fabrics, and commoners were stuck with drab colors like gray and brown. Color is one of the reasons the pau brasil tree in Brazil is now a threatened species.

Exploitation of the pau brasil began in 1501 after Portuguese explorers first set foot on the landmass now known as Brazil. Seeking natural resources for their king, explorers met Brasileiros—indigenous people who collected pau brasil wood to make a red dye. The dye—a shade like the red of glowing embers—was ideal for coloring textiles. The explorers sent log samples home and commercial harvest began, the trees so valuable they had to be defended against sea pirates. The newly discovered land was plundered for this valuable tree, and by the eighteenth century tree populations were already falling.

A rare, slow-growing species, pau brasil trees are only native to Brazil's threatened Atlantic Coastal Forest—an isolated tropical rainforest, originally about twice the size of Texas. Today only about 15 percent of the original forest remains. The pau brasil, also called pernambuco, prefers low-lying coastal areas with well-drained soils and open forest—woods where trees are not crowded too close together. Typically a medium-sized tree, pau brasil may grow 50 to 60 feet (15 to 18 meters) high and achieve a trunk 3 feet (1 meter) in diameter. Although a protected species, the pau brasil is still being harvested illegally.

The pau brasil grows stalks of deep yellow flowers, with one splash of red. They open at dawn and bloom for one day. Bees, attracted to the sweet-smelling blossoms, pollinate the flowers, which evolve into oval-shaped seedpods. The woody seedpods hang empty upon the tree after twisting open to release their seeds.

A member of the pea family, the pau brasil grows flat seedpods, about the size of an adult's ear. Small thorns cover the leaves, as well as the seedpods, which contain 2–3 brownish seeds.

TREE FACT

Trees create places that allow different types of vegetation to grow. The pau brasil provides important habitats for orchids, as well as epiphytes—moss, lichens, and other species that grow on plants.

Spines on the trunk make this tree hard to climb.

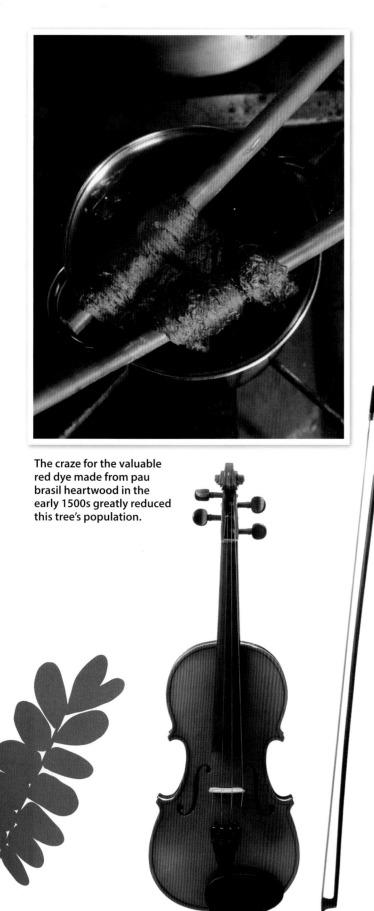

The craze for the valuable red dye made from pau brasil heartwood in the early 1500s greatly reduced this tree's population.

People need pau brasil trees

Indigenous peoples in Brazil, such as the semi-nomadic Tupi, used pau brasil timber to construct tools for hunting and make dye to color cotton fibers. After European traders arrived, the Tupi harvested the logs in exchange for steel swords, axes, fishhooks, and trinkets. Felling trees in the sweltering tropical heat was hard work. They had to remove the bark, section each tree into logs, and transport them from forest to sea. In Europe, a compound called brazilin was extracted from the logs, then used to make dye to color fabrics, clothes, carpets, and curtains. It was also an ingredient in lacquers and ink.

Natural stands of pau brasil were nearly destroyed over the centuries following their discovery by Europeans. In 1875, synthetic dyes made in laboratories began to replace natural dyes, but the devastation of the forests continued into the early 1900s. The tree's durable timber was used in construction, for cabinetry, and to make charcoal.

About two hundred years ago, another use was found for the pau brasil. Its very dense heartwood was discovered to be the best wood of all trees for the art of making top-quality bows for violins, cellos, and other stringed instruments. Each handmade bow draws sound from an instrument in a unique way. Musicians still want the top-quality bows that can only be manufactured from this endangered tree, even though they can cost thousands of dollars.

Great amounts of wood are wasted in the process of making a quality bow. Bow-makers from around the world have come together to help ensure the trees they need will grow into the future. Their organization, the International Pernambuco Conservation Initiative, works to preserve and restore the pau brasil.

Animals need pau brasil trees

The pau brasil's thorny trunk, leaves, and seedpods do not keep all animals away. Bees, butterflies, and hummingbirds have no problem reaching the colorful flower clusters. Bees, believed to be the main pollinators, play an important role in ensuring the survival of this tropical tree. Another visitor, the reddish hermit, is one of the world's smallest hummingbirds. It weighs less than a penny and sports a long, curved bill—ideal for collecting nectar and capturing insects.

The Atlantic Coastal Forest, where pau brasils still grow, is home to an extremely diverse range of wildlife. The colorful blue-throated parakeet is a vulnerable species due to habitat loss, and the purple-winged ground dove is only found in this humid, coastal forest. Other birds include the red-tailed parrot, harpy eagle, and black-cheeked gnateater. Giant antshrikes skulk about the forest, and though these shy birds are experts at keeping hidden, they will emit a ringing call that can be detected a mile away.

Another big-mouthed resident, the brown howler monkey, can be heard 3 miles (5 kilometers) away! These monkeys want members of other monkey troops to know that "this part of the forest is taken!" Other mammals living in this wooded habitat include golden lion tamarins, brocket deer, and woolly spider monkeys.

Males howl to mark their troop's territory, a practice that saves them from wasting energy fighting with other monkeys over habitat.

Like other hummingbirds, the reddish hermit's tongue is forked and covered with hair-like structures called lamellae that help trap nectar.

When you plant a pau brasil, you improve the chances that this nearly extinct species will survive. As well, the rainforests where they grow store immense amounts of carbon and release great amounts of oxygen. This is why rainforests have earned the nickname "the lungs of the planet."

Tall-stilted Mangrove
(*Rhizophora apiculata*)

The native range of the tall-stilted mangrove extends from India to tropical regions in the western Pacific and northern coast of Australia.

I magine living in a place where twice a day saltwater rushes up and over your legs. With each wave, the waterlogged soil beneath your feet swirls about your toes like water fighting its descent down a drain. Kite-worthy winds buffet you about, first trying to pull you one way, then the other. This is the environment where mangrove trees live.

The word mangrove can mean either a single tree, or an entire forest of trees and smaller plants—all able to survive in coastal mudflats, salt marshes, and tidal estuaries. Mangroves grow in tropical regions, including sheltered seashores around much of Australia. The thirty-six different mangrove species there grow in soft mud, along shores where ocean waves are not too large.

Mangrove trees have adapted to thrive in saltwater and airless soil, an ecosystem most land-loving plants can't endure. The tall-stilted mangrove copes with the daily high tide by growing a specialized support system of pitchfork-like roots that erupt from the trunk and branches to anchor into the soil. These air-breathing prop roots, also called stilt roots, graft together in a crisscrossing latticework that prevents the tree from toppling over when water erodes wet soil. Tall-stilted mangroves can live along the sea because specialized tissues in their roots and lower limbs prevent them from absorbing much of the salt in the water.

A medium-sized, fast-growing evergreen, tall-stilted mangroves can reach up to 100 feet (30 meters) and grow trunks 1.5 feet (50 centimeters) in diameter. Each creamy white flower forms a brown fruit about an inch (2.5 centimeters) long that looks like a miniature upside-down pear. The fruit is viviparous—a fancy way of saying that the seed germinates and begins to grow into a seedling while still attached to the tree. The growing part is the root, which looks like an extra long string bean. Each fruit produces one seedling, which is not released for up to three and a half years.

Average height: 100 ft. (30 m)

The tall-stilted mangrove's rough bark is brown, dark gray, or black; its pointy green leaves are leathery.

Growing in pairs, the creamy white flowers are up to half an inch (1.5 centimeters) long.

TREE FACT

All trees are adapted to live in particular environments. Tall-stilted mangrove seedlings get a head start in life by beginning to grow while still attached to the parent tree. By the time the seedling is ready to drop, it can quickly root into the soil. In fact, if the pointy root of the seedling drops straight into the mud, it can plant itself!

Some fish and prawns live beneath tall-stilted mangroves during their juvenile stage before migrating to the open ocean. In Queensland, Australia, about 75 percent of commercially caught fish and prawns depend on mangroves for survival.

People need tall-stilted mangrove trees

Walking alongside a mangrove forest after sunset, you might imagine tall-stilted mangrove trees are plant-style aliens that just might chase you on their leg-like prop roots. It's a good thing their roots keep them firmly anchored, for these trees provide coastal regions with much-needed protection. When wind gales and violent storms erupt, mangroves hold soil in place, reduce pollution from stormwater, and shield shorelines from erosion. The prop roots offer another human benefit by providing an ideal environment for mariculture—the practice of raising prawns and other edible marine creatures in their natural environment.

Tall-stilted mangroves are harvested for lumber and firewood. Although not very durable, the lightweight wood has been used for poles and rafters in fences, huts, and shelters. A useful timber when waterproof wood is needed, the tall-stilted mangrove forms foundation pilings, troughs, and poles for crab traps. Its prop roots and heartwood are most prized for making charcoal. Heavy and dense, charcoal made from the tall-stilted mangrove produces a constant heat with very little smoke.

Mangroves can benefit regional economies because tourists are interested in visiting these unique environments. Travelers come to see these forests up close and observe the wildlife that thrives there. Unfortunately, mangroves have been destroyed through clearing and dredging for agriculture, tourist resorts, and other development. Oil spills, chemicals that leach from litter, and human visitors who trample plant life also threaten this habitat.

Sometimes called the walking fish, mudskippers can change colors to camouflage against enemies.

An upside-down jellyfish waves its tentacles from the mangrove seabed.

Animals need tall-stilted mangrove trees

Imagine wandering along a boardwalk through a mangrove, where creatures lurk above and below the water. Some live here year round, while those like the banded sea krait—a sea snake—only show up with the high tide. In Australia, you might spot wallabies, bandicoots, and other mammals in mangroves, but water rats are more common. They forage underwater for insects, mussels, frogs, and other aquatic life.

Don't be surprised if you see a fish on a branch! Mudskippers are amphibious fish that only live in mangroves and can even climb trees. Able to walk, climb, and leap out of the water, they can survive on land thanks to specialized fins that help them move and skin that allows air breathing. Mudskippers make their way around the mangrove, eating insects and small crustaceans while trying to avoid hungry enemies—snakes, shorebirds, and saltwater crocodiles. Crocs will think you're tasty, too, so keep well back from the water. Nesting on the mangrove's edge, adult crocodiles seek crustaceans, small mammals, and birds, while their young slip into the brackish water to hunt crabs, prawns, and mudskippers.

Mangroves provide an important place for migratory birds and shorebirds to feed and roost. You might spot collared kingfishers nesting there. They use their large bills to capture crabs and fish, and then kill their prey by beating it against a branch. The black bittern, a solitary bird, roosts in the mangrove, occasionally plunging down to capture a fish.

When you plant a tall-stilted mangrove, you help protect a shoreline from the effects of erosion caused by climate change, an important advantage as global warming causes cyclones to occur more often and sea levels to rise. If you visit a mangrove forest, help save its trees by not walking or driving on this sensitive habitat at low tide.

Baobab
(Adansonia digitata)

Baobab trees are native to the semi-arid regions of Africa.

Average height: 60 ft. (20 m)

An African legend describes the dismay the first baobab (BAY-uh-bab) tree felt upon seeing its reflection in the water. Comparing itself to the beauty of the other trees, the baobab realized its leaves were puny, its flowers only white, and its bark like an old elephant's wrinkled skin. The baobab complained to the creator, who did not appreciate this protest and responded by lifting the tree up and slamming it back into the ground, upside down.

With branches that look like tangles of roots spreading outward near the top of the trunk, the baobab deserves its nickname—the upside-down tree. And while its soft, fibrous bark is unlike the covering over any other species, being different is a good thing. The baobab's barrel-like trunk contains spongy fibers that have the unique ability to swell with water and store rain from the wet season. One large tree can hold up to 31,700 US gallons (120,000 liters) of water. In the dry season, the baobab survives by dropping its leaves and living off this stored water.

At heights of up to 60 feet (20 meters), baobabs are not exceptionally tall, but their massive trunks can grow up to 30 feet (10 meters) in diameter. If you could stretch a measuring tape around the Sunland Baobab, one of the largest baobabs in South Africa, you would need a tape 154 feet (47 meters) long. Even though older trees continue to grow, they become hollow, some with enough room to hold at least 60 people inside!

The baobab's bark is so fire resistant, the inner part can be burned out without killing the tree. Wind won't beat this tree either. Baobabs that blow over or are cut down continue to grow because their roots send out new shoots.

Baobabs live without leaves for as long as nine months of the year, then undergo a dramatic change in appearance during the wet season. Leaves appear when the rains come, but flowers bloom at different times during the year. Large, white, and waxy, the flowers hang from the tree like pendulums and emit a rotting scent that attracts bats for pollination. The flowers grow large egg- or cucumber-shaped pods with woody outer shells covered in yellow-brown hairs. Some say the pods, called monkey bread, look like dead rats hanging by their tails, giving the baobab another nickname—the dead rat tree.

Legend says a lion will eat you if you pick a flower from the baobab. The flowers, which open at night, only bloom for about 18 hours. After flowering, fruits take five to six months to develop.

TREE FACT

Because old baobab trees become hollow, their age cannot be determined by counting growth rings. Scientists have used carbon dating to learn that baobab trees can live more than 1,000 years.

The dry, fibrous pulp inside monkey bread contains many reddish-brown seeds, about half the size of a kidney bean.

Baobabs, which are considered a good omen, serve as meeting places in many African communities. Hollow trees can be enlarged by scooping the slimy pulp out of the trunk, which can be done without killing the tree.

People need baobab trees

According to legend, now that the baobab tree is upside down and no longer able to see its reflection, it tries to make up for offending the creator by being helpful to people. Most would say it's doing a good job, for people have found uses for every part of this tree.

Large baobabs, which become hollow with age, have hosted shelters from houses to barns. Baobabs have served as prisons and bus stops, and held churches, pubs, and flush-toilet stalls. The hollow trunks can be used to store water or keep hives for beekeepers. Sometimes considered sacred, baobabs have even been used as burial sites. In some places, cutting down baobabs is illegal, and tradition in certain African cultures forbids destroying them. As a result, baobabs still grow in areas where most other trees have been harvested.

In Africa's dry areas, baobabs provide a very welcome source of food. Young, protein-rich leaves can be eaten like a vegetable, or dried to make a green powder to flavor sauces. Slightly acidic, monkey bread pulp might be sucked on when fresh, cooked with cornmeal, or added to milk or water for a tart drink. The pulp can be used as a substitute for cream of tartar—an ingredient used in baking—while baobab seeds can be ground into flour or roasted for snacks. The seeds also contain edible oils used for cooking. Every part of the baobab has been used to make traditional medicines. In fact, some people believe you can help ensure a baby's health by bathing the child in water in which young baobab roots have soaked.

Elephants seeking food and water can damage baobab trees.

Wahlberg's epauletted fruit bats use their long tongues to extract nectar from baobab flowers.

Animals need baobab trees

Peering out from a hollow baobab tree gives you the perfect chance to get close to wildlife. This tree is as good to animals as it is to people. It provides hollow crannies for hiding, fruit and nectar for food, and branches to hold nests. Each tree is an entire ecosystem, helping to support a variety of life.

The relationship between the baobab tree and the Wahlberg's epauletted fruit bat is symbiotic—they depend on one another. Adapted to open at night, baobab flowers grow on the ends of long stalks near branch tips, where bats can reach them. The flowers provide bats with nectar to eat; the bats serve as pollinators. Hollow trees also provide bats with roosting sites—if you hide inside a baobab during the day, expect to share the space!

Inside that baobab, you might also have to dodge an elephant tusk. During Africa's dry season, elephants eat baobab bark and pierce the tree's trunk with their tusks to reach water. Bushbabies, or galagos, rest in the hollow trees during the day and then feed on baobab flowers at night. Chimpanzees smash open the football-sized monkey bread and devour the seed-filled fruit. Passing through an animal's digestive system helps the seeds spread and germinate.

Nesting birds like Dickinson's kestrel and the whitehead vulture make their homes in baobab trees. Fischer's lovebirds are also found there, but they'd better watch out! Another tree dweller, the 6 foot (1.8 meter) long, venomous boomslang snake patiently waits on a branch hoping to capture a bird or chameleon. Maybe you should exit that tree!

When you plant a baobab, you plant a tree that might provide people and animals with food and shelter for hundreds to thousands of years into the future.

Silk Cotton
(Bombax ceiba)

Silk cottons are native to countries from India, South China, Taiwan, and Myanmar (Burma) to Vietnam; from the Philippines to Papua New Guinea and Australia.

If you're lucky enough to find yourself among silk cotton trees, the beauty of the plentiful red flowers will draw you close. But spiny thorns on the trunk and young branches remind you: this tree is not for climbing! The spiky growths also keep herbivores away. As they age, silk cotton trees lose their spiny weapons and widen at the base to form buttresses 16 to 20 feet (5 to 6 meters) high. The older tree's thick bark helps protect it from fire.

The first two-thirds of a silk cotton trunk is bare, then wide-spreading branches erupt in whorls. Large, waxy, cup-shaped blossoms that are rich with nectar grow on or near the ends of the tree's branches. The flowers, about the size of a coffee mug, are usually deep crimson. They last only a few days, then begin to turn into woody, egg-shaped fruits.

The fruit grows rapidly for about a month, reaching about the length of a banana. Inside, fine, silky cotton encases smooth, oily black seeds. Once ripe, the pods burst open, and the slightest breeze transports the cotton and its seed-passengers long distances through the air to new ground.

Silk cottons are a fast-growing species and can reach heights of up to 130 feet (40 meters) and diameters of up to 7 feet (2 meters). Known as the King of the Forest, it is also called the red-cotton, red silk cotton, and Semal tree. Although it's a tropical species that prefers warm monsoon forests, silk cotton trees are drought-resistant and able to grow in dry areas. In grassland or dried wetland, they serve as a pioneer species—the first plants to appear and grow well on open ground or ground that has been disturbed by grazing, clear-cutting, or fire.

Average height: 130 ft. (40 m)

Two to three weeks after blooming, the satiny petals fall to the ground and form a red carpet.

TREE FACT
Some tall tree species like the silk cotton grow buttress roots to help support their height and prevent them from toppling over. These roots also expand the area where nutrients can be absorbed from the soil.

The specialized buttress roots look like ridges that flare from the lower part of the trunk.

People need silk cotton trees

Humans and silk cotton trees share a long history. Tribal communities in India have found ways to use almost every part of the tree to make medicines and have gathered its roots, stems, and bark to treat snakebites and scorpion stings. The Garasia tribe, however, considers the silk cotton a "god tree," which means that using any part of it is forbidden.

In India, people taking part in a festival called Holika Dahan have a tradition of burning silk cotton wood, a custom that is harming tree populations in some areas. People have also burned its wood for fuel, collected its leaves for animal fodder, and enjoyed shade beneath its branches.

Oil from silk cotton seeds can be used to make soap and lubricants.

The white or pale-pink wood of the silk cotton tree is soft, light, and easy to work with. A favorite for making matchsticks, silk cotton has also been used to build matchboxes, packing cases, shingles, toys, veneer, and plywood.

The dense fiber in silk cotton pods—called kapok—can absorb ten to fifteen times its weight in water and has also been used commercially. Although too short for spinning into yarn, the soft, strong, buoyant, and water-repellant floss has been used in life preservers, as a packing material, and as stuffing for pillows, sleeping bags, and upholstered furniture. The floss, which does not conduct heat, can be used in soundproofing and to insulate refrigerators.

The jungle owlet perches in silk cotton trees.

Indian crested porcupines live in pairs or small groups but usually forage alone.

Animals need silk cotton trees

Pull out a pair of binoculars and try to identify the many birds that use the silk cotton. You'll notice each species visits this tree for a particular reason. Some come to drink the water that collects in flowers or to eat seeds. Others want to roost or nest. You might spot a rose-ringed parakeet nibbling a flower petal, an oriental magpie-robin feeding on nectar, or a purple sunbird gathering soft cotton to line its nest.

The silk cotton tree needs birds, as well as bats like the Indian flying fox. These animals transfer pollen from blossom to blossom, ensuring that the flowers turn into seed-bearing fruit. Feeding birds often knock flower petals or even whole flowers to the ground, but nothing is wasted. Northern palm squirrels, sloth bears, and four-horned antelope arrive to feed on fallen petals. The Hanuman langur eats leaves, as well as flowers.

The blossoms that survive turn to fruit, but animals still come to feed. The Indian crested porcupine eats both ripe and unripe seedpods. Once pods burst open, porcupine, deer, and mice seek out the seeds.

An important member of the tropical ecosystem, the silk cotton also serves as habitat for rock bees and other honeybees.

When you plant a silk cotton tree, you plant an umbrella tree species—one that a large number of animals use for food and habitat. You might also help increase the population of the endangered white-rumped vulture, which favors this tree for roosting and nesting.

Camphor Laurel
(Cinnamomum camphora)

Camphor trees are native to Japan, China, Taiwan, and northern Vietnam.

The camphor laurel is one tree you could recognize with your eyes closed, as long as you could smell a few bruised leaves or a bit of exposed wood. Its timber and leathery foliage release the scent of camphor—the same compound that gives a pungent, nasal-clearing menthol scent to ointments for chest colds. Produced in the tree's wood and bark, camphor can only be extracted with heat. Harvesting involves cutting down branches or entire trees, chipping the wood, then steaming the chips to collect and process the aromatic vapor. In China, leaves and wood are harvested from camphor trees without killing them by a practice called coppicing—cutting a tree or shrub close to the ground to encourage new growth.

A valued evergreen tree native to Southeast Asia, the wide, glossy green leaves of the camphor laurel provide much-appreciated dark shade in the tropical and subtropical regions where it originates. As an introduced species in many countries, camphor laurels are considered a nuisance tree in some places—such as Australia, where they choke out native vegetation. Also known as gum camphor, true camphor, Japanese camphor, and Formosa camphor, this species can live for over 150 years.

Camphor laurels can grow up to 98 feet (30 meters) in their natural habitat and achieve an impressive girth of nearly 8 feet (2.5 meters). Its sturdy branches form round to umbrella-shaped canopies. The rough, deeply furrowed bark is grayish brown; the tiny, fragrant flowers are white to pale yellow. Spring bloomers, the tiny flowers emit a scent that attracts mosquitoes and flies. The pollinated flowers develop into green, pea-sized growths that look like berries but are really pitted fruits, called drupes. Ripening to a dark blue or black, each fruit contains only a single seed, but one large camphor tree can grow more than 100,000 seeds every year! Fruit-eating birds spread camphor laurel seeds to new ground in their droppings.

Average height: 98 ft. (30 m)

Camphor is found in all parts of the tree but is most concentrated in the root.

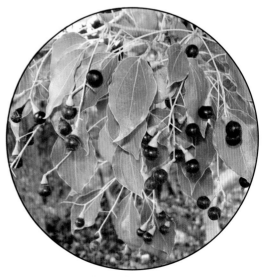

Camphor laurel fruit remains on the tree into the winter.

TREE FACT

As you can see by the camphor laurel's scientific name, *Cinnamomum camphora,* this tree is related to the cinnamon tree—the small evergreen whose bark provides us with the spice used in cinnamon buns and so many other delicious foods.

People need camphor laurel trees

Achoo! Camphor products can be used to slow down your runny nose, keep mosquitoes and lice away, and ease growing pains. People sometimes put camphor in their shoes to make sweaty feet smell better! It's a popular ingredient in a variety of modern-day medicinal products, but people have been using camphor oil since ancient times, when it was administered to stop headaches, encourage sleep, reduce fever, and treat parasites, toothaches, itching, and flatulence. It was an ingredient in embalming fluids used to preserve the bodies of ancient Egyptian mummies and is still used in embalming today. If you had lived during the fourteenth-century bubonic plague epidemic—known as the Black Death—you might have used camphor to clean wounds or try to kill pests to protect yourself from disease.

Today, most camphor oil used in commercial products is created by artificial methods instead of by harvesting trees. Found in perfume, soap, deodorant, incense, paints, and explosives, it is also useful as a plasticizer—a chemical added to rubber and other products to make them stronger, more flexible, and easier to work with.

A fine-grained wood, camphor laurel has been harvested for its timber and used to build furniture, coffins, and fretwork—carved or patterned wood. Because moths, ants, and other insects dislike its aroma, camphor laurel is ideal for building furniture where clothes are stored, like chests, cabinets, and wardrobes.

It's hard to appear royal when you're swatting flies. In India, camphor was used to make kings' thrones because it kept away insects (except for termites). Notice the wood's multicolored stripes and silky sheen.

Animals need camphor laurel trees

Suppose you were to visit a treehouse built high up in a camphor tree in Japan. You just might run into a Japanese giant flying squirrel! This arboreal species lives in broadleaf or mixed wood forests where camphor trees grow among cedar, zelkova, and oaks, such as the chinquapin. Mixed forests provide the diversity most animals need to meet their needs. As well as feeding on camphor tree fruits, this giant flying squirrel spends its nights seeking leaves, buds, seeds, flowers, bark, and cones from other trees in the forest. Large eyes help the squirrel see in the dark as it glides from tree to tree and finds a place to hide away in tree hollows or branches—always on the lookout for enemy weasels, martens, and red foxes.

As you make your way down the tree, watch for mice running upside down along the branches. Japan is the only country where the Japanese dormouse is found. Extremely agile, it runs along the underside of tree branches using its curved, hinged claws and cushiony paw-bottoms to hold on. What's a Japanese dormouse doing in a camphor tree? He's looking for fruit, insects, bird eggs, and other treats.

You decide it's time to climb down to the ground, but your foot pushes into something furry. It's a Japanese macaque. Also called snow monkeys, they use the low branches of the camphor laurel for sleeping and also visit the tree to feed on its fruit.

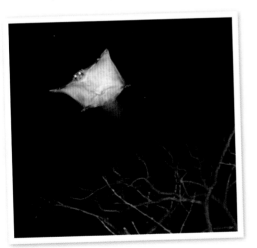

The Japanese giant flying squirrel inhabits large camphor laurels.

As a nocturnal species that hibernates, the Japanese dormouse is not easy to spot. This species is designated as a Natural Monument in Japan, which means the national government monitors the preservation of its habitat.

When you plant a camphor laurel, you plant an attractive shade-producing tree that can tolerate drought and smog. Camphor laurel is best planted in its native region due to its ability to invade other environments and out-compete native species.

Scotch Pine
(*Pinus sylvestris*)

Scotch pines have a large natural range that extends from Scotland to Siberia, above the Arctic circle in Scandinavia, and to the south of Spain.

Here's a tree you might spot both inside and outside a window. Indoors, it stands upright in a container of water, sparkling with colored balls, garlands, and tinsel. The Scotch pine has sturdy branches and keeps its needles over the holiday season, making it a popular choice when it comes to Christmas decorating. While young Christmas trees grown on tree farms are cone shaped because of the care they receive, wild trees that reach maturity may grow multiple trunks with wide branches, or a single trunk that stands straight and tall.

Scotch pines can reach up to 120 feet (36 meters) high and be as wide as 8 feet (2.4 meters). A spring-blooming species, it grows male and female cones on the same tree. Wind blows pollen from the clusters of yellow males to the rosy-purple females, which develop into green cones that take two years to mature. Turning brown with age, the scales on the egg-shaped, woody cone spread open when the weather is warm and dry. When conditions are good, more than 3,000 cones might grow on a single Scotch pine. One cone may hold up to twenty-five seeds that the wind will scatter to new ground.

The most widespread conifer species in the world, Scotch pines grow from sea level up to 8,000 feet (2,400 meters), sometimes thriving in habitats that other species can't endure. A long-living tree, Scotch pines often live up to 300 years, though trees as old as 700 years have been discovered. Also called Scot's pine, it is the only conifer native to Scotland, a country home to large pine forests before most of its trees were harvested for fuel, cleared for farming, or overgrazed by sheep and other livestock. The legendary Caledonian Forest in the Scottish Highlands is the only native pine forest in Britain. Although once a vast woodland, very little of it remains.

TREE FACT

When a Scotch pine dies without falling over, the trunk may stay upright for 50 or even 100 years because resin in the sap slows the rotting process.

Average height: 120 ft. (36 m)

The blue-green needles point away from the trunk, while cones point toward the trunk. The tough, pointy needles turn yellowish-green in winter but stay on the tree for two to three years before dropping off in the autumn.

As a Scotch pine ages, cracked, gray bark replaces some of its orange-brown bark.

Depending on the climate, it can take six to twelve years for a potential Christmas tree to reach a good size for harvesting.

People need Scotch pine trees

See if you can detect a hint of pine next time you sniff a candy, pudding, or frozen dairy product. Fragrant oil distilled from Scotch pine needles is used to flavor food and beverages, and also to make disinfecting detergents and other cleaning products. Pine oil may be found in bath products, shoe polish, and paint thinner.

The fresh smell of newly cut Scotch pine planks can make carpenters inhale deeply with pleasure. Strong and light, top-quality boards are used to make furniture, while lower grades are made into products like pallets—wooden platforms often used to store and transport materials in warehouses. You might walk through a doorway framed in pine, place your clothes in pine drawers, and sit at your pine desk to write on paper made from pine pulp.

Appreciated for its resistance to water, Scotch pine timber was once favored in shipbuilding. Its trunk has been tapped to collect resin for making tar and turpentine, and its inner bark used to make rope. Known as the king of the forest, the Scotch pine was once planted on the graves of chiefs and brave warriors.

As well as being raised on Christmas tree farms, Scotch pines are planted for windbreaks and as ornamental trees. The most widespread pine species and an introduced tree in Canada and the United States, the Scotch pine is naturalized in some areas, meaning it has become like a wild species that spreads without planting.

Modern-day woodworkers appreciate the Scotch pine's ability to soak up preservatives, which makes it a durable choice when building roofs, decks, fences, and telephone poles. The timber becomes a rich yellow to red color when finished.

Animals need Scotch pine trees

A hungry bird versus a Scotch pinecone. The seeds, tightly enclosed beneath the pinecone's green scales, should be safe. But wait! This bird is a Scottish crossbill, able to use its crossed bill like tweezers. Landing on a cone, the crossbill pries the scales apart with its beak. Sticking its tongue into the cone, the crossbill flicks a seed down its throat.

Found only in Scotland, the Scottish crossbill depends on Scotch pine seeds for food. Along with the parrot crossbill and common crossbill, it nests in the Scotch pine, choosing large, old trees to brood its young. Crossbills also share the Scotch pine with capercaillie (KAP-er-KAY-lee), a turkey-sized European grouse that shelters on low branches.

Scotch pine forests provide habitats for badgers and foxes, as well as the European pine marten, a declining species in Britain. The pine marten nests in hollow trees and hunts red squirrels in the treetops. Red squirrels, with tails almost as long as their bodies, use their fantastic ability to balance to leap away through the branches. Never far from their food supply, these squirrels build multiple nests of dried grass, moss, and twigs in Scotch pine. Their habit of hiding seeds helps new trees grow.

The Scottish crossbill depends on its native pine habitat.

Scottish wood ants feed on sawflies, a pest that feeds on pine needles during its larval stage.

When you plant a Scotch pine, the environment is improved by this tree's ability to reduce erosion—it grows in dry areas where other species cannot survive. Wildlife benefit from year-round shelter.

Cork Oak
(Quercus suber)

The cork oak is found in southwestern Europe and northwestern Africa. It grows in Portugal, Spain, France, Italy, Morocco, Algeria, and Tunisia.

Average height: 65 ft. (20 m)

No matter where you live, there's a very good chance that bark from a cork oak tree is somewhere in your home. It is used to make wine stoppers, baseballs, and coasters. Cork can be found in computer printers, helmets, and car soundproofing. It is even used in airplanes and the space industry!

The cork oak tree is famous for its unique outer bark. Light and elastic, it can be compressed to make many different products. The thick bark is also very resistant to forest fire. Cork oak trees have deep root systems that help them survive the western Mediterranean area's hot, dry summers and cold, moist winters.

An evergreen, the cork oak grows spiny green leaves, twisty branches, a thick crown, and an annual crop of small chocolate-brown acorns. Cork oaks can reach 65 feet (20 meters) high and more than 7 feet (2 meters) in diameter. They are slow growers but can live as long as 250 years.

The best thing about the cork oak is that its bark can be harvested without killing the tree. It takes fifteen to twenty years before the first crop of cork is thick enough to be removed. Workers use special knives to carefully peel the thick outer bark. After being stripped, the tree grows a new layer of cork. It can be peeled every nine to twelve years for 150 to 200 years. Cork is a renewable resource, with a single tree giving about 400 pounds (180 kilograms) of bark each time it is harvested. That's a stack of cork that would fill two bathtubs and weigh as much as a refrigerator!

Cork is an environmentally friendly product because it is biodegradable and recyclable. In Portugal, cork oak trees are considered a national treasure, and it is illegal to chop down any tree that can still produce usable bark. Portugal calls the cork tree the sobreiro (sub-BRAY-uh). Its forests produce more cork than any other country.

One tree can yield enough cork to make 25,000 wine stoppers each time the bark is stripped.

A scaly cap covers half the acorn, which ripens from green to brown.

TREE FACT

In rural North Africa, cork has been identified as a product that, if properly managed, will create sustainable jobs for local communities.

Cork oak planks are stored outside for about six months because weathering improves the quality of the cork. Afterwards, planks are boiled for at least one hour to make them clean and bendable. After another three weeks of drying, the planks are ready to be trimmed and sorted.

People need cork oak trees

People have used cork for thousands of years. Artifacts found at Greek, Roman, and Egyptian archeological sites show cork was used as a plug to seal olive oil and wine in amphorae—wide-mouthed pottery jars. Early Greeks also used it to make sandals, while as early as 3,000 BCE people in China and Egypt used cork to make floats for their fishing lines. Since the time of the ancient Greeks, generations of parents have taught their children how to harvest cork from trees.

Today, workers in the western Mediterranean remove about 300,000 tons of cork oak bark each year. Most of it is used to make wine stoppers. Harvest takes place in late spring and early summer. The cork collected during a tree's first two harvests is too hard to be made into wine stoppers, which are made of only the best quality cork. The first harvests provide cork that is better suited for making flooring or insulation.

In North Africa, cork has been used for firewood and to make charcoal for heating and cooking. In some countries, cork oak is planted as an ornamental tree. Its roots reduce soil erosion and help soil retain water. Cork oak can be grown without using fertilizers, herbicides, or irrigation.

Cork is a product that can last from decades to centuries without rotting. Cork scraps are used for insulation and other construction materials, so no harvested cork is wasted.

Animal life is good for the cork oak trees, too: European jays, squirrels, mice, and even dung beetles bury acorns to eat later—some of these acorns will sprout into trees.

TREE FACT

By providing food and habitat for many types of life, cork oaks help ensure biodiversity—an environment with a variety of plant and animal species. Biodiversity is important to keeping ecosystems healthy and ensuring all life forms can survive. Some birds—like the white-rumped swift and the blackcap—*only* live in cork oak forests.

Moroccan spadefoot toads, like this one, share cork oak woodlands with geckos, frogs, skinks, and snub-nosed vipers.

Animals need cork oak trees

Imagine visiting a cork oak forest in the Iberian Peninsula of Spain and Portugal. You lean against a trunk's rough gray bark and close your eyes. A squirrel scolds from an overhead branch. A lapwing chirps a gentle melody. Something heavy-sounding snuffles nearby. Better lift your lids—you don't want a wild boar to find you instead of the acorns he smells!

It's often easier to find traces of animals than the critters themselves. A careful search might reveal tracks from hare, fox, mongoose, roe deer, or genets. Birds are often simpler to spot, with more than a hundred species of songbird found in some cork oak landscapes. Tree crowns provide shelter for black storks, buzzards, short-toed eagles, and bee-eaters. Migrating and overwintering birds crossing through northern Europe and Africa depend on cork oak forests.

Six million wood pigeons and 70,000 common cranes feed on cork oak acorns in the Iberian Peninsula every year. Counting them would keep you busy for a long time!

Two animals in the forest are much harder to count. That's because they're endangered. The Iberian lynx is closer to extinction than any other large cat in the world. The Spanish imperial eagle also struggles to survive. These animals use the cork oak habitat to nest, rest, and hunt.

When you plant a cork oak tree, you plant one of the trees best able to absorb carbon dioxide from the atmosphere.

Downy Birch
(Betula pubescens)

Downy birch grows naturally throughout most of Europe, northern Asia, Iceland, and Greenland.

The elegant downy birch may have fine branches and small leaves, but this is one tough tree. It can survive poor soil, wind, high altitudes, and hard frosts. The downy birch can even withstand air pollution.

All trees that grow in the far north tend to be short and stunted, but downy birch survive farther north than any other broadleaf species on Earth. They grow up to 6 feet (2 meters) high in the icy Arctic, but can reach up to 65 feet (20 meters) high and around 2 feet (60 centimeters) in diameter in other areas.

This amazing tree marks the northern timberline—a line trees don't live beyond because the growing season is too short and the landscape is too windy and exposed. The downy birch is believed to have been one of the first trees to put down roots in the rocky soil after the glaciers of the last ice age retreated. A subspecies called the Arctic downy birch is the only forest-forming native tree to grow in Iceland and Greenland.

The downy birch gets its name from the short, soft, furry hairs that grow on new twigs. It is also called hairy birch, bog birch, and mountain birch. This tree may grow several trunks, or only one. Its papery, peeling bark may be gray-white to red-brown, with horizontal markings that look like random dashes. The wind-pollinated flowers of the downy birch are arranged in catkins, sometimes called lamb's tails—which is just what they look like! The flowers on one mature tree produce up to a million seeds each year, but only a few become new trees. Those that survive usually live between 60 and 90 years—not very old for a tree.

The hardy downy birch is a pioneer species—one of the first plants to grow after grazing, clear-cutting, or fire disturbs land. Birch stands encourage both plant and animal biodiversity. Their branches and leaves allow enough light into the forest for other plants to grow. The downy birch is a nurse species—a plant that provides shelter to slower-growing vegetation.

Average height: 6–65 ft. (2–20 m)

Catkins are clusters of flowers that contain scaly leaf-like structures called bracts. The downy birch grows male and female catkins on the same tree.

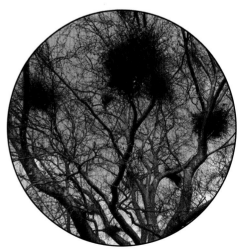

Downy birch trees often grow a distorted tangle of closely packed twigs called witches' broom. A fungus triggers the growth, which looks a bit like a bird's nest at the top of the tree.

TREE FACT

In Canada, the northern timberline has served as a geographic and political boundary. When Europeans first came to Canada, Inuit lived above the timberline, while other indigenous peoples lived below it. Today, climate change is causing the timberline to shift.

In North America, indigenous peoples have used various species of birch to make canoes, teepee coverings, and clothes from bark. They even used the waterproof bark to make pots that could be placed over a cooking fire!

You might find birch plywood inside your home if you have a guitar, a set of drums, or a keyboard. You might find it beneath your feet if you are a skateboarder, or in your hands if you use toothpicks or make model aircraft!

People need downy birch trees

The wood of the downy birch is pale, smooth, dense, and strong. It can be used as a building material to make furniture and plywood. In Finland, downy birch is harvested to make pulp for paper.

Downy birch is believed to have medicinal value. People in some countries consider it healthy to drink birch tea or birch sap, which is pale green, watery, and a bit sweet. Trees can be tapped for their sugary sap in the spring to make a thin syrup or brew into beer or wine.

Birch is said to represent love and protect you from the evil eye. Long ago, cradles were made from birch to protect babies from wicked spirits.

About sixty species of birch exist, and early cultures found these trees to be very useful. A broken arm was repaired by placing the injured limb into a cast made of birch bark, first soaked in hot water. The bark was also used for tanning leather. Birch wood was used to make spoons and other kitchen utensils, as well as handles for tools. Tree trunks were placed as pathways across bogs, and piles of birch were used to make steeplechase obstacles for horses. Birch twigs were tied around a stick to make a besom—a broom for outdoor sweeping. This was the kind of broom witches were said to fly!

When you plant a downy birch, you plant a tree that might one day be used to make the paper in a book. The tree you plant might also warm someone on a winter day. Birch burns hot because it is so dense, and it can be lit even when frozen, thanks to oil inside the wood. Often, though, downy birch is simply planted for its beauty.

In winter, moose graze on young downy birch twigs.

Animals need downy birch trees

The downy birch is the best tree for putting up with harsh Arctic conditions, so it's no wonder it's popular with animals in the far north. Moose, deer, and hare browse on its shoots. Birds, mice, and other animals eat its seeds. Insects come to its flowers. The insects attract bats, which come to nest and roost. The peeling bark found on birch trees provides a perfect habitat for bats, insects, and small birds looking for places to hide.

If you walk through birch woodland, expect to pick your way through undergrowth. The plants in your way provide habitat and food for many species, so try not to crush them. Perhaps you can find an animal path to walk on. Just watch out for other animals using the trail! In Finland, the brown bear, reindeer, wolf, fox, lynx, and wolverine are just some of the animals that use birch woodlands. Do you hear any tweets or warbling? In Ireland, siskins, finches, and redpolls depend on downy birch seeds for their winter diet.

As you step over fallen logs and see dead trees still upright, remember that even a dead birch benefits wildlife. Grouse use deadfall in courtship displays, and woodpeckers and other species nest in tree cavities. Rotting logs also provide important habitats for insects and other invertebrates.

Redpolls, like this one, depend on the downy birch for food.

Cedar of Lebanon
(Cedrus libani)

The cedar of Lebanon is native to Syria, Lebanon, and Turkey.

Average height: 60–114 ft. (18–35 m)

Running your hand along the dark, furrowed bark of a cedar of Lebanon tree is like touching history. The Sumerians, an ancient civilization, wrote about cedars more than 5,000 years ago, and the ancient Greek author Homer mentioned them in *The Iliad*, a famous poem written over 3,000 years ago. Cedars of Lebanon are even noted in the Bible. These texts, the earliest written records of any tree, show the historical importance of this magnificent species.

A member of the pine family, the cedar of Lebanon is an elegant evergreen found in mountainous areas up to elevations of 7,200 feet (2,200 meters). It can grow a massive trunk, nearly 8 feet (2.5 metres) in diameter, and reach heights of 60 to 114 feet (18 to 35 meters). When a cedar of Lebanon tree grows in an open area, its branches spread so far, it may grow almost as wide as it is tall. Deep roots enable this tree to resist drought. It can also tolerate frost, but it will not survive winters that are too cold or last too long.

Wind causes male cones to release great amounts of pollen, fertilizing the female cones that will eventually release papery, winged seeds. When mature, the cones, 3 to 5 inches (7.5 to 12 centimeters) long and 1.5 inches (4 centimeters) wide, grow upright on branches.

Once plentiful, the cedar of Lebanon is rare in its native habitat—Syria, Lebanon, and Turkey. It has been nearly loved to death! The last 5,000 years have seen this species heavily logged for its sweet-smelling, insect-resistant wood. Natural stands have been harvested for fuel, and feral goats have over-grazed the young saplings that might have formed new forests. Regrowth is slow for many reasons. It takes twenty to forty years before a cedar of Lebanon produces seed-bearing cones. The trees only grow cones every second year, and when they finally appear, there are not a lot of them. Fortunately, this species can live a long time. Some cedars of Lebanon are believed to be 2,000 years old.

Reforested land must be protected from grazing goats.

Barrel-shaped cones grow upright on the tops of branches.

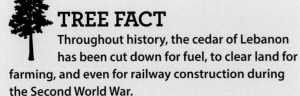

TREE FACT
Throughout history, the cedar of Lebanon has been cut down for fuel, to clear land for farming, and even for railway construction during the Second World War.

These cedars thrive in places that are difficult for humans to access.

People need cedar of Lebanon trees

As one of the "most wanted" timbers in history, the cedar of Lebanon once served as a status symbol. Kings and other notable people wanted the best quality wood for their building projects and coveted the cedar of Lebanon for its strength, handsome grain, and long-lasting fragrance. The Old Testament in the Bible reveals that this easy-to-work-with wood was made into planks, pillars, and beams for temples and palaces.

Resistant to rot and insect attack, its logs were raised up as supporting beams for large buildings and ship masts; lumber was used to build houses, civic buildings, navy ships, and tombs. Exported to Egypt and other places, cedar resin was found suitable as a medicinal ingredient, for caulking ships, and for the embalming of Egyptian pharaohs.

Some historians say the great cedar of Lebanon forests began to disappear in the sixth century. During Lebanon's civil war, from 1975 to 1990, more deforestation occurred. Today, less than 3 percent of Lebanon's original cedar is believed to exist. In some regions, such as Turkey's Taurus Mountains, cedars of Lebanon survive because they grow on hard-to-access mountain slopes.

Animals need cedar of Lebanon trees

They come to roost, hunt, nest, raise their young, and hide. When a country suffers from vast deforestation, the little habitat that remains becomes even more important to wildlife. Birds like the winter wren forage in cedar forests, favoring beetles but also eating other insects and spiders. The forests also attract finches like the Syrian serin, a vulnerable species due to the impacts of grazing, woodcutting, and drought. If you ever visit a cedar forest, listen for this bird's trilling sounds coming from the top of a cedar. Notice its bright yellow forehead and see if you can spot its nest concealed in the cedar branches. While you're looking up,

try to spot the rebounding branches as a Persian squirrel zooms along. An arboreal species, it nests in cedars and feeds on cones. Even higher up, storks and other migrating birds pass over the forest as they fly between their breeding and wintering ranges.

Below the branches, animals like red foxes, porcupines, wild boars, jungle cats, and golden jackals take advantage of the forest habitat. Very rarely, a wolf might wander past, but their populations are small and wolves are stealthy creatures, making them hard to spot.

Wild boars are often able to thrive in conditions unable to support less adaptable wildlife.

Hoopoes, which breed in cedar forests, protect themselves by squirting fecal matter at their enemies.

When you plant a cedar of Lebanon, you plant a tree desired by ancient royalty. The cedar of Lebanon will always be valued for its timber, but the greatest part about planting this tree is knowing that you're helping to keep a vulnerable species alive.

When you save a tree

One of the easiest ways to help save a tree is by reducing your use of new products that come from forests—especially wood, cardboard, and paper. With a little creativity, you will find all kinds of ways to do it. Instead of buying new lumber, you could make a tree house or doghouse from a torn-down fence. Instead of seeing cardboard as just another item for the recycling bin, look at it with the eyes of an inventor. You could turn boxes into model rockets, lemonade stands, sleds, or forts. Rather than buying craft supplies, you could reuse paper to make papier-mâché decorations, jewelry, or masks. Try making scratch pads out of paper sheets that are no longer needed. You might even reuse greeting cards. Start a new tradition with your friends by sending the same card back and forth every birthday or holiday.

It's easy to reduce your use of new paper. Try setting wider margins on computer documents you need to print, and only make hard copies when absolutely necessary. Make a habit of printing and writing on both sides of paper.

When buying books, check if they are printed on forest-friendly or recycled paper. You can also buy books secondhand or borrow them from a library.

Every effort you make to reduce waste matters. Paper that ends up in a dump rots and creates methane—a strong greenhouse gas twenty times more damaging than carbon dioxide.

Magazines can become bowls, cardboard can become bracelets, and tissue paper can become flowers.

HOW DO TREES MAKE YOU FEEL?

If you are obsessed with being around trees, you might be said to have dendromania. If you are afraid of trees, you might have dendrophobia.

Plant a tree

Every tree you plant creates animal habitat and helps slow global warming.

The best species to plant is one that grows naturally where you live. Collect seeds from fruits, nuts, or cones, then choose a spot where a tree will have enough room to grow. Push your finger into the soil about 1 inch (2.5 centimeters) deep and plunk the seed into the hole. Cover it with soil until the ground is almost level. Mark the spot with a stick, water the seed, and give it time to grow. Write down the date your tree appears and watch how it changes over the years. See what animals come to the tree, and be proud that you have helped provide animal habitat, cleaner air, and a beautiful sight to behold—a tree!

TREE FACT

If you plant a seed that doesn't grow, try again in another place. Or better yet, plant several seeds in different areas and see how many come up. Sometimes seeds don't sprout because the soil is poor, the seed gets too little or too much water, or other plants choke out the seedling or block the sun. Just keep trying!

57

Trees and animals need each other

When you save a tree, you help members of an ecosystem stay in sync. Just as each tree is important to wildlife, animals are important to trees. Insects and birds pollinate flowers and help spread acorns and seeds. Earthworms burrow among tree roots and improve the transfer of air and water through the soil. Mammals prune trees when they eat branches and enrich soil with the droppings they leave behind. There is even value in old trees that fall to the ground and dead trees that still stand. They provide vital habitats for the small animals and insects that larger predators feed upon.

Almost the size of a crow, pileated woodpeckers, like this one, make rectangular holes in dead trees. Owls, ducks, bats, and other species use abandoned holes for nesting. You can tell what kind of woodpecker has chiseled into a tree by the hole's shape, size, and height.

Japanese macaques, also known as snow monkeys, eat camphor laurel fruit. They help new trees grow when they spit out seeds or leave them behind in their waste.

Find animal signs

Next time you see a tree, check for animal signs like insect galls, branches with ragged edges, or missing strips of bark. Look up into the limbs for a bird's nest or woodpecker hole, then down to the ground to see whether squirrels have discarded piles of cone scales beneath the tree. You might find sawdust left by beetles, leaves full of insect holes, or bark scrapings. Listen for bees buzzing around flowers, a robin defending its territory, or a deer snorting. Remember that trees are busy places at night, too. At dusk, listen for the howl of a coyote, the hoot of an owl, or chirps of singing insects like crickets, grasshoppers, or katydids.

Insects create galls, like the fuzzy ones here, as mini-habitats.

Scientists aren't certain why bears leave scratch marks on trees like this trembling aspen. It may be to indicate territory and therefore avoid conflict.

Wooden rafters help support the High Level Bridge in Edmonton, Alberta. Completed in 1913, pedestrians, vehicles, and streetcars still cross the North Saskatchewan River on this 2,478 foot (755 meter) bridge.

Plants for people

Throughout history, people have depended on trees for survival. Trees provide fruit, nuts, and gum for food; timber for shelter, tools, and fuel; and ingredients for medicines. The active ingredient in aspirin, salicin, was discovered in the white willow, while quinine, used to treat malaria, was processed from the cinchona tree.

Trees have enabled people to accomplish incredible feats like building ships to navigate oceans, bridges to span rivers, and railway lines to cross vast continents. Today, forestry is big business, but trees offer even more than the products we already depend upon. New medicines, especially in the world's tropical rainforests, await discovery. Trees capture carbon dioxide in the atmosphere, helping counter the effects of greenhouse gases. Perhaps one of the closest-to-home benefits of trees is the way they make people feel. Trees bring a sense of peace. Astronauts have said that not being able to go outside and enjoy nature is a difficult aspect of living in space. With so many benefits and so much potential, saving a tree means ensuring human comfort, safety, and survival.

Around the world, people are coming together to tackle the effects of deforestation. In 2007, when he was nine years old, a boy in Germany named Felix Finkbeiner started the Plant-for-the-Planet Foundation with his friends. Since then, more than 12 billion trees have been planted in 193 countries. The foundation's goal is to see 1 trillion trees planted by 2020. That equals roughly 150 trees per person on Earth!

Taking Action!

- The International Tree Foundation organizes tree planting that restores habitats, improves soil quality, and creates jobs that help combat poverty in rural Africa. It also delivers a program in the United Kingdom that encourages young people to become Tree Guardians.

- In India, Grow-Trees encourages people to increase the many benefits trees provide by planting trees instead of giving gifts.

- Tree Canada funds projects to plant and care for trees at schools and in communities. It encourages Canadians to celebrate National Tree Day on the last Wednesday of September.

- Countries around the world celebrate Arbor Day—a time set aside to plant and appreciate trees.

- Green Legacy Hiroshima has been established to safeguard and spread worldwide the seeds and saplings of Hiroshima's A-bomb survivor trees. After the Japanese city was devastated by an atomic bomb on August 6, 1945, only about 170 trees were left in a 1.2 mile (2 km) radius from ground zero.

Glossary

arboreal — relating to trees, or found in trees.

biodiversity — the variety of plant and animal species in an environment.

boreal forest — northern forests that mainly contain coniferous trees.

canopy — the uppermost layer of branches in a forest, or, less often, on a single tree.

clear-cutting — harvesting all of the timber in an area of forest at one time, a method of deforestation.

climate change — long-term changes to weather patterns around the world, including changes in precipitation, winds, and temperatures. Global warming is one aspect of climate change.

coniferous trees (conifers) — trees that grow cones and usually produce leaves that are needles.

crown — all of a tree's twigs, branches, and leaves. The crown's shape, which may be rounded, conical, spreading, or another form, changes as the tree grows.

deciduous trees — species that grow broad leaves each spring and drop their leaves in the autumn.

deforestation — clearing an area of forest of all its trees, usually by clear-cutting or burning.

ecosystem — a place where plants and animals interact with each other to live and grow.

endangered — a species at risk of becoming extinct throughout most or all of its range.

epiphytes — plants like mosses and lichens, which sprout on host trees, taking moisture and nutrition from air and rain.

ethnobotany — the science that explores indigenous peoples' use of plants.

evergreen — a tree with foliage that remains green throughout an entire growing season.

fossil fuel — a natural fuel—such as coal, natural gas, or oil—that is formed from the remains of plants or animals.

global warming — a climate change phenomenon that occurs when the Earth's atmosphere traps warm air around our planet and causes temperatures to rise, and snow, sea ice, and glaciers to melt.

greenhouse gases — carbon dioxide and other heat-trapping gases that collect in the atmosphere and contribute to global warming through the heating of the Earth's surface and lower atmosphere.

growth ring — the layer of wood formed in a tree during one growing season.

habitat — the place where a plant or animal naturally lives.

heartwood — dead sapwood that has become old, hard, and resistant to decay.

naturalized species — a species that is introduced to a region and then spreads into the wild, so that it is able to successfully reproduce without additional planting.

nitrogen cycle — the natural process by which nitrogen, necessary for life, passes from the air and the soil to plants and animals, then back to air and soil.

phloem — the inner bark that transports food made by the leaves to the rest of the tree.

photosynthesis — the process by which green plants take in light, water, and carbon dioxide and turn them into the food they need. Light energy is converted into chemical energy, as the tree takes in carbon dioxide and releases oxygen.

pioneer species — the first plants to appear and grow well on open ground or ground that has been disturbed by grazing, clear-cutting, or fire.

pollen — dust-like and usually yellow particles in a flower that wind or insects carry to other plants of the same species to fertilize seeds.

pulp — a material that can be made from wood to create paper products.

rainforest — a woodland in a tropical region with a high yearly rainfall, where very tall, broad-leaved evergreens create a continuous canopy.

renewable resource — any resource that occurs in nature—such as water, wood, or plant oils—that can be replaced over time through cycles in nature.

resin — a sticky yellow or brown substance made by some trees. It is often used in the manufacturing of varnishes, solvents, and adhesives, although synthetic versions of the substance are more commonly used today.

sap — the watery solution of dissolved sugar, salt, and minerals that moves through a tree's tissues to transport nourishment to the roots, trunk, branches, and leaves.

sapling — a slender, young tree.

sapwood — living wood that stores food and transports sap upward from the roots.

symbiotic — a relationship in which two different organisms live in association with each other and depend on one another.

threatened species — a species that is at risk of becoming endangered throughout most or all of its range.

timberline — a line beyond which trees don't live, because the growing season is too short and the landscape is too windy and exposed.

transpiration process — the process in which water is drawn up through a tree's roots and evaporates through its leaves.

umbrella tree — one that a large number of animals use for food and habitat.

undergrowth — plants that grow along the forest floor and provide habitat and food for many species.

windbreak — a group of shrubs or trees that reduce the force of wind.

Index

Photo Credits

6: © George Ostertag/MaXx Images; 9 (top right): © European Press Photo Agency B.V./Alamy; 15 (bottom right): © Clarence Holmes/ MaXx Images; 18 (top): © Dinodia/MaXx Images; 18 (bottom right): © dave stamboulis/Alamy; 19 (top left): © Greg Dimijian/ Science Source; 19 (top right): © Doug Wechsler/MaXx Images; 20: Mauroguanandi/Creative Commons; 21 (top right, bottom right): Mauroguanandi/Creative Commons; 22 (top left): © BrazilPhotos.com/Alamy; 23 (top right): © Gabriel Rojo/naturepl.com; 23 (bottom right): © Nick Athanas; 25 (bottom right): © blickwinkel/Alamy; 27 (bottom left): © Reinhard Dirscherl/Alamy; 29 (top right): © Ton Rulkens; 30 (top): © Steffen & Alexandra Sailer/ardea.com; 31 (top right): Dorling Kindersley/UI/MaxX Images; 34 (top): Image Broker/FLPA; 36: © Mixa/Alamy; 37 (top right): © Peter Titmuss/Alamy; 37 (bottom right): Public Domain/Creative Commons; 39 (bottom left): © Gouichi Wada/Minden Pictures; 39 (bottom right): © Nature Production/naturepl.com; 40: D. u. M Sheldon/ MaxX Images; 42 (bottom right): © Johner Images/Alamy; 43 (top right): © Paul Hobson/FLPA/MaxX Images; 43 (bottom right): © David Whitaker/Alamy; 45 (bottom right): © itanistock/Alamy; 48: © A. Laule/MaxX Images; 49 (bottom right): © E.A. Janes/ MaxX Images; 51 (top right): © Mark A Johnson/MaxX Images; 58 (bottom): © Jeremy Woodhouse/MaxX Images; 59 (top right): © Stephan Pietzko/MaxX Images; 59 (bottom right): Michael Short/Let's Go Outdoors; 60 (top): Marcel Schoenhardt/Creative Commons; 61 (top left): © Jeff Greenberg/Alamy; 61 (top right): ©KidStock/MaxX Images; 61 (middle left): © Richard Levine/Alamy; all other photos royalty-free (Dreamstime, iStockphoto, Shutterstock, BigStock).

Acknowledgments

Just as it takes many trees to make up a forest, it takes numerous talented individuals to create an engaging book. My heartfelt appreciation goes to the staff at Owlkids, who nurtured my idea to write a children's title that explores the fascinating ecological and social significance of tree species from around the world. Particular thanks to Jessica Burgess and Jennifer Stokes for the fine editing skills they applied to the manuscript. It is extremely rewarding to work with people who examine each word choice with consideration for both readers and the author. Thanks also to Samantha Edwards, Jaleesa Scotland, and Alisa Baldwin, designers who played the important role of ensuring an attractive book for readers, as well as Tracey Jacklin, who located the best photos to illustrate the importance of trees. My gratitude extends to Robert Guy, professor, Department of Forest Sciences, University of British Columbia, a tree expert who kindly and thoroughly reviewed the content. Finally, thanks to the individuals and organizations around the world who plant trees and promote tree appreciation.